THE TALE OF A PERCEIVED WOMAN

IN 8 QUESTIONS

SHALINI KAUSHIK

Copyright © Shalini Kaushik
All Rights Reserved.

ISBN 979-888591434-5

This book is dedicated to:

My grandparents, three of whom I've recently lost in the pandemic

My mom and dad for being my strength

My brother who has always pushed me to come out of my comfort
zone

My closest friends who hold me tight in this crisis and celebrate
my success

And my professors and dear students for believing in me

Contents

Contents

Contents

Preface

Perception is one-sided. It may be unfiltered and raw, but it often thrives on opinions–mostly the unfounded kind. And the subject never really has any say in it.

In a male-dominated society, there are always glaring differences between society's perception of a woman's selfhood and the intrinsic identity that she has always wanted to build. The moment she is born, she has to become the kind of woman the society demands. While she undergoes a series of trials throughout her formative years, she encounters certain behavioural patterns, certain misogynistic and inhumane actions that are considered 'the usual' in the eyes of the society. Since these actions are not to be spoken of and therefore slid under the carpet, these revelations naturally needed to be read–not spoken–in
the form of this book.

Through this book of poetry, I have attempted to encapsulate these perceptions in the form of 8 questions–questions which you must have encountered in your day-to-day life.

The first section: "Why can't we understand you?" talks about the relatable experience of being misunderstood–by your family, peers and strangers alike.

The second: "Why can't you be like...?" explores gendered notions conditioned in both sexes since childhood along with their later manifestations during their adult lives.

While the third: "Why can't I choose?" depicts the lose-lose situation of women in aspects of love and career, the fourth section: "Why'd you do that?" exposes the horrifying trauma-inducing actions on women caused by the male gaze and female objectification.

The fifth section: "When will they realize?" goes on to talk about the various physical and mental health issues often faced by women, that are generally disregarded. Be it cervical pain, menstruation or a UTI, their basic needs somehow turn into a constant struggle for survival.

The sixth: "Why are you here?" is a blatant revelation of the restrictive practices directed at the progressive woman in the workplace.

The woman, vilified, objectified and besmirched, will now take her stand. "Is it my turn now?" therefore becomes a befitting answer to the crippling measures of the patriarchal society that previously held her back. In true Kintsugi fashion, the woman embraces her scars and reshapes her broken self into someone that matches the identity she has always believed in.

The final section, "Do you know?" is my personal message to all the persevering women out there. A clear movement from poetry to prose, this is where I beseech you–find yourself for you are not alone. You have never been alone. There will be situations when you'll feel helpless, and that's completely okay. These poems, mostly anecdotal in nature, are a testament to the resilience that you and I have exhibited.

Because the perceived woman is not just me. It is us.

1. Why can't we understand you?

1. Black salt is an emotion.
Be it papaya or lemonade or watermelon
or raita,
your mother would stick to it
and sprinkle it on top.
But that's not the way
I make it.
2. Adulting is like
putting up a WhatsApp status
and forgetting
to see
"seen".

2. Why can't we understand you?

3. She didn't know which was the toughest -
answering dumb questions or
dicing a banana.

4. ~Womb~
Her father belonged to Uttar Pradesh,
and he settled in Delhi after his posting.
Her mother's roots traced back to Uttar Pradesh,
despite her being born and brought up in Madhya Pradesh.
Now although they both settled in Delhi
and ensured she was born and brought up
in the same city,
she had to eventually leave the womb for her job and
latch on to her mother's home state -
Madhya Pradesh -
for her connection to her mother's womb still remained
tangible and
present.

3. Why can't we understand you?

5. Pollution

Her heart always longs for Delhi
but her body longs for MP.
Her soul is caught between the two,
for she hasn't been fully released
from her cocoon yet.

6. What described her best was her favourite drink -

coconut water
(not native to her home city) -
hard on the outside,
smooth inside.

4. Why can't we understand you?

7. ~Immigrant~

She didn't have to go to the U.S. or U.K

to feel like an immigrant.

She went from a metro city

to a small city.

That was enough for the

coveted immigrant experience.

8. No matter how many arguments you win at work,

you will never win one

at home

with your maid.

5. Why can't we understand you?

9. ~Single men~

Just because she can speak in fluent English

in a city where it isn't common,

you need not imagine her as the mother of your kids.

10. ~Sisterhood~

Happiness for her is

when her female friends

take the throne.

6. Why can't we understand you?

11. ~Bus seats~

The palpitating anxiety and joy of

saving DTC bus seats

for her girl gang,

on her way to college

12. ~Smile~

She smiles at you.

Do not take it for a 'Yes'

unless she uses words to express it.

7. Why can't we understand you?

13. ~Dark chocolate~

The only companion

which stays with you

in the darkest of times

14. ~Foundation course~

While preparing for a class on tenses,

life seems nowhere near

Present Perfect or

Future Perfect

8. Why can't we understand you?

15. ~Bags~

Teaching in an age where

a professor's bag is heavier

than a student's

16. ~Shallowness~

The shallowness

of doing a PhD,

just to use 'Dr'

in front of their names

17. ~Marriage material~

The grossness of manufacturing,

packaging and selling women

as marriage material

in the markets

is disheartening.

9. Why can't you be like...?

1. ~Besan~

A six-year-old tells her to put besan for a fairer skin

and to remove hair from her upper lip,

because girls cannot be dark and hairy.

2. ~City~

The city she lives in is safe

because

girls and women stay at home after sunset.

10. Why can't you be like...?

3. ~Academia~

When an academician says,

"No one is fairer than me here,"

you are already one of them.

4. ~Chores~

A female colleague said,

"Aurato ke kaam toh aurato ko hi karne hai"

(Women have to do women's work.)

11. Why can't you be like...?

5. ~Space~

You ask her to sit with her legs closed.

You ask her to occupy the littlest space.

Why?

Because she is a girl.

Because she is a woman.

She wishes she could strike you hard

while screaming:

Patriarchy!

Sexism!

Misogyny!

6. ~Pink~

While a lot of her girl friends were seen in pink frocks,

she never harbored the same conception.

Her father's favorite colour was pink;

so she believed it must have been quite popular -

because she could see it in the women's coaches

in metro trains,

and the DTC tickets specially reserved

for someone like her.

Pink autos were introduced,

pink toilets were constructed.

She loved 'Pink' the movie but
couldn't digest its marketing,
where the king-sized portrait of Amitabh Bachchan
occupied most of the space
in the huge banners while the three female leads
were made to fit in a
comparatively smaller and tighter space.

12. Why can't you be like...?

7. She was tired of her strawberry legs.

Therefore, she couldn't wear what she desired.

Beauty standards had told her so for the past decade.

8. She wonders how the exposed midriff in a saree is not

problematic

whereas denims with kurtis are.

9. ~Society~

She was 28

and her biological clock was ticking.

13. Why can't you be like...?

10. ~Barbie~

When she was young, she wasn't given a Barbie;
Barbie was a privilege to have.
Her parents weren't well-off enough to afford that.
She got her first Barbie in class sixth,
not because it symbolized dolls for girls but
because she too was a product of capitalism.
She wanted to experience what it felt like to be privileged.
That Barbie didn't attract her much.
It was for sure her first and last.

14. Why can't you be like...?

11. ~Age~
The whole obsession with
not asking the age of women
(it's taboo);
and the whole obsession with
women not telling their age:
she asks why?

12. ~Not like other girls~
The appreciation that
comes by putting other women
down

15. Why can't I choose?

1. ~Trophy wife~

She was asked to be a trophy wife

because his profession mattered more.

She called it 'quits'

and was thus cursed to stay forever alone.

2. ~Scam~

You lied to her.

You faked all the appreciation.

You acted all liberal and progressive.

You were a scam she struggled with.

3. She cried the whole night

and then naturally, wore a brave smile

and went to work in the morning.

Who knew her heart was too heavy for her to hold.

16. Why can't I choose?

4. She was told, "I love you."
Thus began a project that would soon
culminate with her identity erased.
5. She was told she won't be judged,
and yet she was -
each day, each night.
She was told she won't be stopped,
and yet she was -
each day, each night.
She was told to adjust;
she couldn't.
Each minute, each second,
she felt caged and lost.
Each microsecond and millisecond,
she argued and protested:
She was the bad woman.
6. ~She read fairy tales~
And then misogyny
happened.

17. Why can't I choose?

7. As a girlfriend,
she was strong and independent.
As a wife, she was too bold and assertive.
(says the husband)

8. ~Past~
She was labeled a prostitute
because she had a past.
Her grace and sincerity were questioned
because she had a past.
Her dedication and loyalty were questioned
because she had a past.
But didn't she have to grow up
because she had one such past?

18. Why can't I choose?

9. ~Veil~

Asked to be worn in front of the elders,
and now, she is the *devi*.
She let it slide off her face;
now, she is the *chudail*.

10. ~Blessings~

The *bichiya*
said to her, "I would save your husband."
The *mangalsutra*
said to her, "I would save your husband."
The *chudi*
said to her, "I would save your husband."
The *nath*
said to her, "I would save your husband."
The *sindoor*
said to her, "I would save your husband."
She asked them, "Who is going to save me?"
They said to her, "*Sada suhagan raho*".

19. Why can't I choose?

11. At 19, she encountered Wollstonecraft.

At 25, she couldn't encounter equality in marriage.

Was it all mere words?

12. ~Discarded~

It was winter.

Her mother was asked to remove her socks.

"Thank God! She doesn't have a flat foot,

otherwise her bad luck would have destroyed the family."

The question changed when it came to her daughter:

"Are you a virgin?"

Alas! She was made to feel discarded.

13. When work called Kiara to go abroad for a week,

she packed her bags, told her mother and went.

Her mother couldn't apply this principle to her life;

because she had learnt the language of silence

while her father learnt the language of dominance.

20. Why can't I choose?

14. ~Convenience~

"Hey! You need to wear suits and sarees in front of my family and shorts and skirts at the parties with me."

15. We don't take dowry but

you may give whatever you want to.

16. ~Hollow~

Only when she had turned hollow within,

did she realize she had made enough bad decisions.

She now feared to open her heart to another one.

17. ~Unpaid chores~

When your dads end up asking

your moms:

"What do you do the whole day?"

21. Why'd you do that?

1. ~Finger~

She was just four;

he was eight.

Supposedly, her parents made her call him '*bhaiya*'.

Their parents chit-chatted in the other room

while he made her sit in her balcony with lights off and her

legs wide open

and inserted his finger inside her.

She didn't know what was happening because

no one taught her to differentiate between

good and bad touch.

When she grew up,

her vocabulary widened with words like

'molestation' and 'harassment'.

But it was too late!

2. ~Salesman~

A salesman asked her about the neighbours

next door.

She answered him well;

he put his hand around her waist

and delivered a peck.

She was confused.

Maybe, because she was

just eight.

22. Why'd you do that?

3. ~Jhumkas~

At 11,

excited for her first jhumkas:

Little did she know that the jhumkas would come

at the cost of her pinched waist in

the crowd.

4. ~Molester~

She was now in college.

Her vocabulary knew concepts like molestation.

While catching a bus for her college,

her neighbour, Sukanya, a girl of her age

was entering the building.

He followed her.

Sukanya didn't notice because

she was engrossed in her music.

Sukanya was safe because he didn't follow her.

But the moment the other girl exited the building

and boarded the bus,

he tried to swiftly brush past her,

while groping her breast.

She kept on making frantic calls to her father,

but he never reached on time.

23. Why'd you do that?

5. ~Metro~

At 18,

she was interning with a reputed company.

It was 8 PM, Dec 30th, 2011.

She had a male friend along,

and thought she'll be safe with him.

But alas! The crowded metro separated them and

she ended up in a coach full of men,

where one of them kept on squeezing her breasts even

over the double-layered sweater.

6. ~DTC~

She was lucky enough to get a seat

in a crowded DTC bus.

While returning from college,

she loved the window seat because that made her feel safe.

Unfortunately, that day,

she found the seat next to it,

only to feel a man's fingers

working their way

towards her breasts.

7. ~Bra strap~

Because she has breasts.

24. Why'd you do that?

8. ~Landlady~

The landlady instructed her

to put a cotton chunni

over her wet undergarments,

when they were put out for drying

on the terrace.

9. ~Marital rape~

He forces her to lie down.

She begs him to not remove her gown

while he breaks her will

bit-by-bit.

10. ~Pain~

The pain of being scanned

each day

from breasts to bottom.

25. Why'd you do that?

11. ~Abuse~
Even the Hindi abuses
didn't leave our women
and their vagina
in peace.

12. ~Thin waist~
The whole obsession
with a thin waist
is prevalent in Indian songs.

26. When will they realize?

1. ~The difference~

She was 28:

it was the beginning of her cervical.

Although she loved dancing,

she had to take a break

from it.

When she recovered,

Covid hit her again.

She braced that alone

while being away from home.

She came home after the recovery,

thinking she was back in shape

to pursue what she loved the most;

However, she got a UTI,

and before she could begin the treatment,

she had:

Periods. Exclamation! Interrobang?!

2. ~Away from home~

It took a virus to make her realize

what home truly was.

27. When will they realize?

3. ~Patriarchy and academia~

Household chores are unpaid work for the woman of a family.

She doesn't get paid for making up her home

because the patriarchy says,

"That's her duty!"

A professor's worth is determined by

their publications and not the classes they take.

Seems like they both need to take those sessions

on mental health.

4. Clean female washrooms are a far cry,

because no one cares.

She drank less water,

and controlled her pee,

because her workplace didn't have a clean washroom

for women.

5. ~Periods~

Judging her for praying to God,

while on her periods.

Not letting her touch the pickle jars

while on her periods.

Not letting their maid cook

while on her periods.

28. When will they realize?

6. ~Not depression~

She couldn't get out of bed.

No! Please! It wasn't depression.

She couldn't face the light.

No! Please! It wasn't depression.

She braced herself for class only to cry later.

No! Please! It wasn't depression.

She went to bed again hoping the sun doesn't rise the next day.

No! Please! It wasn't depression.

7. ~Woman to woman~

Her maid said to her:

"You don't LOOK ill;

So, you aren't unwell."

29. Why are you here?

1. At 27,

she was rude because she was straightforward.

She was called the 'clever young girl' from the big city.

She was difficult to be absorbed.

2. ~Urban privileged feminist~

You call her an urban privileged feminist.

She works in a small city;

judgements are passed on her.

She is forced to cover herself with a chunni,

forced to drink from the cup of misogyny.

She is made to feel a misfit

and is the subject of gossip.

Yet, to call her an urban privileged feminist

is convenient, isn't it?

30. Why are you here?

3. ~Threat~

She is a threat

because she knows her role well;

because she is professional in the unprofessional world,

because she is independent in the dependent world.

So, it's only natural that

she should 'settle down' to become one of them.

4. ~Privilege~

She sits with a male colleague in a meeting.

Thus begins her character assassination,

while you ignore

that education and higher positions are still male privileges.

5. She danced her heart out,

only to be laughed at by her male colleagues.

6. ~Promotions~

Please all, question none;

you'll get the promotions.

31. Why are you here?

7. ~Reality~

She needed strength each morning
to hit her workplace,
because the workplace was making it hard for her.
But she couldn't deny that the place was sculpting her
into someone
more mature,
more tolerant.
It made her realize
the more serious issues in life,
the torn shirts of her students,
the struggle they faced in reading sentences
while filling up their forms.

8. ~Reply~

A male colleague who was about to retire once said,
"You are like a daughter to me so
you must wear clothes that aren't tight."
This sugar-coated language was for the fact
that you have breasts, therefore,
you must wear a chunni.
She responded, "The problem isn't in my dress or body;
it is in the male mentality that exists here."
The next day, she wished her workplace father,

but he didn't respond.

32. Why are you here?

9. ~Fire~

When her male junior tried to order her

and question her sincerity at work,

she refused to take it silently

and responded blazingly

through her words and work.

10. When the most educated lot

demands that gender roles be performed,

she comes to the realization

that there was never any relation

between being educated and being progressive.

11. ~Roar~

With each threateningly high-pitched sound

emitted by a male student,

she resolved to become stronger

and announce her presence even louder.

33. Why are you here?

12. ~Neglect~
She allocates some work
to her junior;
while she is talking to him,
he decides to ignore her and
attend his call.

13. ~Mansplaining~
A male colleague
preaches about the benefits of vaccination
but he chooses not to get vaccinated.

14. ~Fragile manhood~
A lot of men feel
talking in a loud voice will
make the women submissive
and
magically turn the men powerful.

34. Why are you here?

15. A male colleague
once said:
"You should know how to cook because
your mother cooked for you;
think of the next ten years from now,
you will have to feed your child."

16. She was asked to 'shut up' by a senior male faculty
and instead listen to her junior
because he was a man.

17. ~Leader~
She came from a culture where
leadership meant doing it yourself first and
set an example of a hardworking leader.
But she is now stuck in a culture
where others believe these leaders
are a convenience -
so, let them do everything
because they can.

35. Why are you here?

18. ~Mourning~

She couldn't meet her grandparents for

the last time,

because

she works in a far-off city

which had the election's code of conduct.

She cried in silence

and mourned for her loss

with no one watching.

19. ~Dry skin~

Just because her dried skin could absorb the oil well

doesn't mean it could absorb your nonsense too.

20. ~Art~

She has finally understood

the art of

seeing the dark hearts

of those smiling faces.

36. Why are you here?

21. She knew how to stop people
when they crossed professional decency
and forced themselves into her personal space.
They soon encountered a barrier of strong communication;
they didn't know outspoken women existed;
their families never had them.
22. ~Single woman~
Being a single woman
at 29,
and living alone in a small city
was tough for her.
She couldn't invite her male friends
at home
without being judged.
23. ~Tribe~
Amongst the toxicity,
she finally found her tribe
in women
and in men.
Her tribe made sure that
she was safe and sound.
A clean heart and sincere work
could indeed perform miracles.

37. Is it my turn now?

1. She sits with her head low
only to pounce back at you
(when it's time).
2. He came, he went.
She was scattered and shattered;
she stayed and stood;
she rode and rose;
he sat and saw.
3. You tried to take away the feminist in her;
you tried to cover her in the garb of patriarchy;
you tried to teach her *lihaz*
and *maryada*.
But did you succeed?

38. Is it my turn now?

4. He said, "It'll be tough for you to stick to your feminist ideals."
She said, "Back off."
5. If he judges you for your past,
he is not the one for you.
Move on.
6. You will break down into pieces;
you will be worn out;
but you will gather those pieces again and
come out stronger.
7. She matured
the moment she accepted
the grey in her hair.

39. Is it my turn now?

8. Despite being broken,
she rose up,
because -
her father cried with her,
her mother hugged her hard,
her brother made her dance,
her friends held her hand,
her professors pushed her to be professionally strong,
and she did the same to her broken students.
The legacy goes on.

9. ~Heaven~
Marriages are made in heaven.
So is domestic violence.
(Your heaven isn't mine to claim.)

10. A woman tells her,
"If your husband allows you to study or work, you are lucky!"
She asks, "How do I compensate if I don't have a husband?"

40. Is it my turn now?

11. ~Aspirations~

She had a stable career,

her aspirations limitless.

One day she wanted to be a writer,

The other day a dancer,

The third day an owner of a café -

She wanted it all.

She was a go-getter.

12. ~No means No~

Where did you find the Yes in a woman's No?

41. Is it my turn now?

13. She was considered dust;
but she is that last speck of dust
which disseminates in the cosmos,
impossible to be trapped in the confines of
your dustpan and bin.

14. ~Rejections~
She cried with her head down.
She had no ideas left for her research.
Her papers were rejected -
that was the beginning of her struggles,
but not the end.
It was purgation
before a new beginning.

42. Is it my turn now?

15. He tried to break her.
She suffered but didn't break.
When he couldn't succeed,
he tried that on another woman.
She suffered too but didn't break,
And the third endured too.
He has failed to make one his prey.
Strong women aren't easy to break
and strong women aren't born strong -
They become one with their experiences
and realize who they've always been -
an impenetrable shield.
16. Before you call a woman 'Feminazi',
keep a check on your casual sexism.
17. If he keeps a tab on your activities,
if he checks your phone each time,
if he forces you to put on marriage markers,
if he advises you each time without being asked for,
if he justifies that he is always right,
if he justifies that you are always wrong -
don't justify him as being protective and possessive.
It is not cute!
It is frustrating.

And it is certainly not acceptable.

43. Is it my turn now?

18. Apparently, it was the caffeine
in her coffee that made her
high and ambitious.

19. She wanted to shout out loud:
- Financial independence and satisfaction need not be related always.
and
- Financial independence does not imply being ready for marriage.

20. Her past was meant to be her past,
not her present
not her future.

44. Is it my turn now?

21. ~Adrenaline rush~

What gives her an adrenaline rush?

Successful ambitious women!

22. ~Instagram~

She loved dancing,

so, she made her Instagram public

and showcased her talent on it.

(She stopped caring

about what her colleagues thought of her.)

45. Do you know?

1. Dear women

If you are encountering hatred from the people around you
and without any reason, that is okay.
Try being pleasant to even the ones who dislike or hate you.
There will come a time when those people will give up
and even if they don't,
it will be their loss.

2. Dear women

If you are worried about getting into your dream institution
for Masters or securing a place in a Ph.D program, I hope you
make it there.
And if you don't, then try finding at least one person
(irrespective of gender) at whichever place you are, who could
motivate you
to move ahead in life. That one person could be a:
friend/professor/teacher
whose influence would make you strive for the best.

46. Do you know?

3. Dear women

If you are going through a heartbreak or a failed marriage, remember

that everything happens for a reason. Compromises are fine from both ends but

if you end up losing your identity with them, they aren't worth it.

Someone broke your heart - it is not your fault if they turned out to be an arse.

It is his loss, not yours. You deserve better and I

wish you the best in that. But there isn't any harm in staying single because

ending up with the wrong person is the worst that can happen to you.

Life is beautiful; make it even more beautiful by converting your weaknesses into your strengths. Some

turned out to be jerks but let us be thankful to all the supportive men in our lives.

Feel lucky if you are blessed with supportive fathers, brothers, teachers, professors, mentors,

or male friends.

4. Dear women

If you are going through minor and major issues in your family, this too shall pass.
Everything has a solution but if it doesn't, just wait for time to subside because
certain things are not in your hands.
Time doesn't always remain the same.

47. Do you know?

5. Dear women

If you are stressed about convincing your parents for the man you want to marry, you

know what?

Many a times, parents are cool with your decisions. But still, if they are not, be

emotionally and financially strong enough for taking your decisions; be strong enough

to handle yourself well and come out of it.

(even if your decision turns out to be wrong.)

6. Dear women

If you have failed in balancing your personal and professional lives, it is absolutely fine -

because the concept of a superwoman is a flawed one and it unnecessarily puts burden

on you. It is okay to fail in order to learn.

48. Do you know?

7. Dear women

If people are trying to put you down in any sphere of life, feel lucky that you are

important to them. You are definitely doing well, therefore others feel the need to put you

down. Keep going. Do not stop.

8. Dear women

If you do not know what's wrong with you and you feel sad for no reason, that's normal.

It happens with most of us at some point in life. It is a phase and it will pass.

During such times and otherwise, always have your go-to women because female bondings really help.

49. Do you know?

9. Dear women

If you inferred that I'm well sorted in life, you've missed the point then. I'm as messed up

as you are. I'm one of you, but together, we shall come out strong along with the help of

supportive women/men/others in our lives. (Healing hugs!)

10. Dear women

You were always forced to find yourselves in Mankind. You were always made to

look for your stories in History. You were always put in peripheries. That can't stop you.

That never has. You are the center. The universe revolves around you. Metamorphosis awaits!

Your voice is the agent which will call for Your Story - a much sought-after narrative

that needs to be a part of Womankind.

Glossary

1. **Raita**: an Indian side dish made with curd, vegetables or boondi

2. **Besan**: a Hindi term for gram flour

3. **Devi**: a Hindu goddess

4. **Chudail**: a witch

5. **Bichiya**: toe ring

6. **Mangalsutra**: auspicious thread with black beads in it

7. **Chudi**: bangles

8. **Nath**: nosepin/nose ring

9. **Sindoor:** vermilion red cosmetic powder worn by women in a Hindu marriage

10. ***Sada Suhagan Raho***: a Hindi phrase used as a blessing by elders to women to always remain married in their lives. It also points towards the longer lives of husbands; dying as a suhagan (married woman) could be intended in the phrase rather than dying as a widow.

11. **Bhaiya**: A Hindi word for 'brother'

12. **Chunni**: A part of an Indian attire called suit. A chunni is like a scarf or stole made with a very thin material. Its purpose is to cover the breasts of women.

13: **Lihaz:** an Urdu word for esteem and respect

14. **Maryada:** Borrowed from Sanskrit, this Hindi word means limit

15. **Dayan**: Hindi word for a witch

Author's Bio

Shalini Kaushik is an Assistant Professor with Madhya Pradesh Higher Education Department and is currently posted at the Department of English, Govt. P.G. College, Guna, M.P. since December, 2019.

She has completed her Ph.D. titled "Aesthetics of Walt Disney Films: A Study in Relation to the Feminist Categories and Conceptualisation" in December 2019 from the Department of English and Other European Languages, Dr. Harisingh Gour Central University, Sagar, M.P.

Her areas of interest include popular culture, cultural studies, literary criticism, feminist literature. She has attended various conferences, seminars, workshops and published a couple of papers. She has also been a member of the Women Studies Development Cell during her college years at Jesus and Mary College, University of Delhi.

She currently teaches Drama, Linguistics and Literary Criticism to undergraduate and postgraduate students. At present, she serves as the officiating head of the Department of English at her college.

The Tale of a Perceived Woman is her debut release.

* 9 7 9 8 8 8 5 9 1 4 3 4 5 *